Africa
Wildlife
3rd Edition

Includes:

Africa Biomes

Habitats and Habits

Bird Activities

Mammal Activities

Reptile & Amphibian Activities

Invertebrate Activities

Wildlife Respect

Waterford Press
www.waterfordpress.com

Introduction

Africa is the second-largest continent on Earth. It encompasses several biomes within its almost twelve million square miles – the Mediterranean biome, desert, savanna, tropical rain forest, montane biome and freshwater biome.

A biome is a large region that has similar plants, animals and organisms that have adapted to the geography and climate of that area. A biome can have several ecosystems.

An ecosystem is a community of organisms that interact with one another and with their environment. Several ecosystems can exist within a biome.

Ecosystems within the major biomes of Africa include woodlands and forests, shrubs and scrublands, a semidesert region, grasslands, wetlands, coastal areas and an oasis within the Sahara Desert.

More than one million species of animals live in Africa, including lions, baboons, warthogs, camels and some of the largest land animals on Earth – elephants and giraffes.

Africa Biomes

Mediterranean Biome

The Mediterranean biome is a region of woodlands, forests and scrublands in Africa that borders the Mediterranean Sea and the Atlantic Ocean. It has dry summers and rainy winters. Animals who live here include the North African hedgehog, the Eurasian otter and several species of bats.

Desert Biome (Sahara Desert)

The Sahara Desert is the largest hot desert in the world and home to about 70 mammal species, 90 bird species and hundreds of species of reptiles. Dangerous animals like the deathstalker scorpion and the venomous sand viper live here. Guelta d'Archei, an oasis in the desert, is home to camels, crocodiles and desert antelope. To the south is the Sahel zone, a semiarid region that forms a transition between the desert and the grasslands of the savanna.

Savanna Biome

The savanna is the largest biome in southern Africa, covering about 46% of its area. Serengeti National Park in Tanzania is known for a large wildebeest and zebra population. Lions, leopards, elephants, hippos and gazelles also live at the park. The savanna is mostly open grassland with very few trees. It is known for extreme wet and dry seasons.

Tropical Rainforest Biome

The tropical rain forest is a hot, moist biome known for vegetation with dense canopies that form three different layers. Rain falls all year long. Most of Africa's rainforests are in the Congo River basin on the Atlantic Ocean side. The forest is home to gorillas, chimpanzees, elephants and a native population of pygmies.

Montane Biome

Africa's montane biome is a moderate to high-altitude area of isolated mountains that border the Rift Valley. The climate is temperate and can get as warm as 86°F (30°C) in the summer. Several species of birds, reptiles and amphibians live here, as well as some larger mammals like the African golden cat and bush elephant.

Freshwater Biome

Africa has many freshwater systems, including the Nile River and the seven African Great Lakes. Lake Victoria is considered the largest tropical lake and the second largest freshwater lake in the world. The hippopotamus, mongoose and Nile crocodile all live in this biome.

Class Act

Animals can be sorted into categories based on certain characteristics. The system for sorting animals into categories is called taxonomy. Mammals, birds, fish, reptiles and amphibians belong to a class of animals called vertebrates. Vertebrates are animals with backbones. Invertebrates are another class of animals that do not have backbones (like insects, worms and spiders).

Draw a line between the African animal and its class.

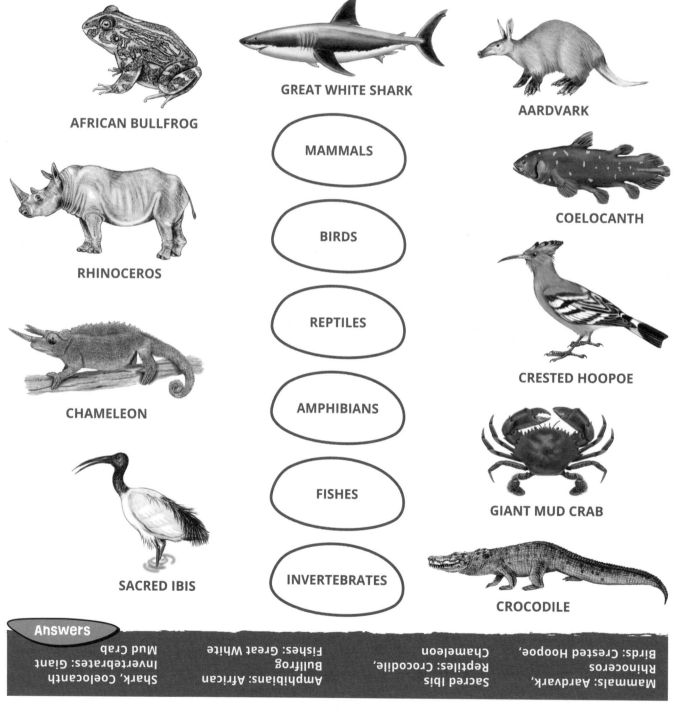

GREAT WHITE SHARK

AFRICAN BULLFROG

AARDVARK

MAMMALS

RHINOCEROS

COELOCANTH

BIRDS

REPTILES

CRESTED HOOPOE

CHAMELEON

AMPHIBIANS

GIANT MUD CRAB

FISHES

SACRED IBIS

INVERTEBRATES

CROCODILE

You Are What You Eat

Herbivores eat mostly plants. Carnivores eat other animals.
Omnivores eat plants and animals.

Draw a line between the African animal and its diet.

GIRAFFE

CHEETAH

STRIPED HYENA

OMNIVORE

CHIMPANZEE

HERBIVORE

BUSHPIG

CARNIVORE

HIPPOPOTAMUS

GIANT EAGLE-OWL

CROCODILE

5

Food Chain

A food chain is the order in which animals feed on other plants and animals. All living things need each other. For instance, a simple food chain might be: cricket to pygmy mouse to owl.

Producers – A producer takes the sun's energy and stores it as food.

Consumers – A consumer feeds on other living things to get energy. Consumers can include herbivores, carnivores and omnivores.

Decomposers – A decomposer consumes waste and dead organisms for energy.

Label each living organism below as a producer, consumer or decomposer.

LION

REED

BEETLE GRUB

ZEBRA

SPOTTED HYENA

DUNG BEETLE

GORILLA

ACACIA

Home Sweet Home

There are a number of habitats in Africa that support a unique community of animals that feed and live there.

**Draw a line between the animal and its habitat.
(Note: Many animals can live in several habitats.)**

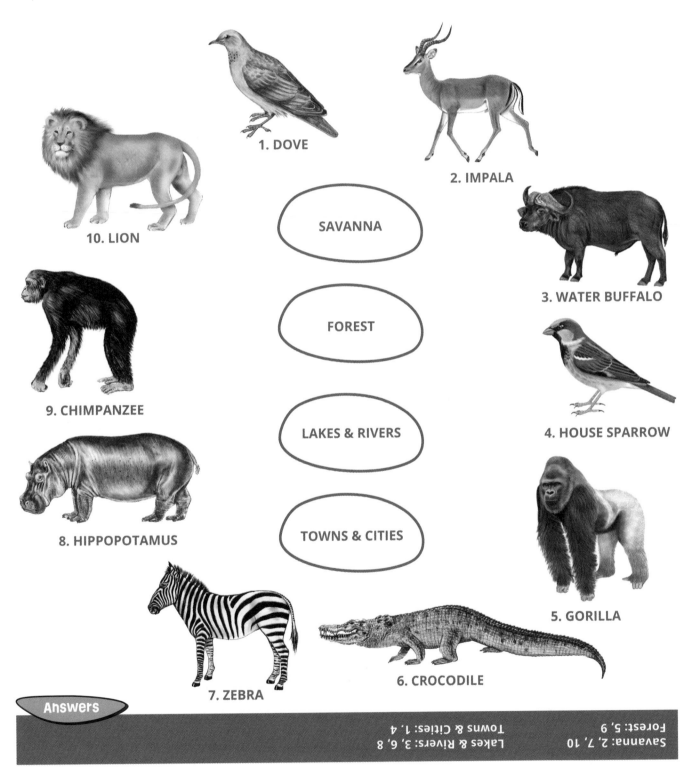

1. DOVE

2. IMPALA

10. LION

SAVANNA

3. WATER BUFFALO

FOREST

9. CHIMPANZEE

LAKES & RIVERS

4. HOUSE SPARROW

8. HIPPOPOTAMUS

TOWNS & CITIES

5. GORILLA

7. ZEBRA

6. CROCODILE

Word Search

Locate these birds of prey hidden among the letters.

```
H R E D F D P G S D N O G M X I
Z B A U G U R B U Z Z A R D H J
M Z A S I F M T C L U J J U S A
G Y B M A H B Z J C R J Y Q M V
H M O B N R A T C T E K X N S C
H E E P T D T Z O U U E C V X R
M P K H E B A V L Z E I T E F O
A Z B O A X L Y X S R P P J I W
G M J O G A E Z D Y Z U N X P N
H N N H L D U F K L E C B U W E
W I Y S E C R E T A R Y B I R D
Q D C H O O D E D V U L T U R E
I R J Y W H C L Z Q Y N K W D A
P O O O L D B G A L G S N X Z G
Q A F R I C A N S C O P S O W L
G E G Y P T I A N V U L T U R E
```

SECRETARYBIRD

HOODED VULTURE

EGYPTIAN VULTURE

CROWNED EAGLE

GIANT EAGLE-OWL

BATALEUR

AFRICAN SCOPS OWL

AUGUR BUZZARD

Answers

```
G E G Y P T I A N V U L T U R E
Q A F R I C A N S C O P S O W L
P O O O L D B G A L G S N X Z G
I R J Y W H C L Z Q Y N K W D A
Q D C H O O D E D V U L T U R E
W I Y S E C R E T A R Y B I R D
H N N H L D U F K L E C B U W E
G M J O G A E Z D Y Z U N X P N
A Z B O A X L Y X S R P P J I W
M P K H E B A V L Z E I T E F O
H E E P T D T Z O U U E C V X R
H M O B N R A T C T E K X N S C
G Y B M A H B Z J C R J Y Q M V
M Z A S I F M T C L U J J U S A
Z B A U G U R B U Z Z A R D H J
H R E D F D P G S D N O G M X I
```

Name Match

Draw a line between the mammal and its name.

1.

ZEBRA

HEDGEHOG

WARTHOG

GORILLA

SABLE ANTELOPE

GAZELLE

LEOPARD

BABOON

2.

3.

4.

5.

6.

7.

8.

Color Me

Use the Color Key to help you color the pictures below.

The **African wild dog's** bushy tail has a white tip that may help it stay in touch with its pack while hunting. No two wild dogs have the exact same marks.

Color Key

Known for its loud calls, the **great blue turaco** is native to the forests of central and west Africa.

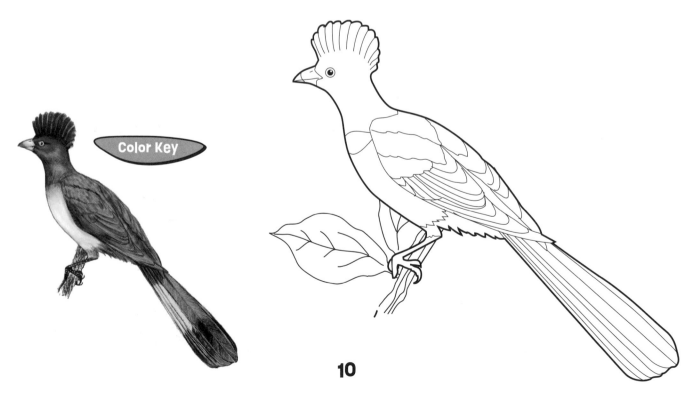

Color Key

Who Am I?

Name these African mammals.

1. My name comes from ancient Greek meaning "river horse."

4. I use over 30 sounds to communicate, including barks, grunts and howls.

2. I am also known as a gnu and am one of the most common African hoofed animals.

5. I am the fastest land animal in the world and can reach speeds of 75 mph (120 kph).

3. I have thick skin, a prominent horn and can weigh over 2,000 lbs. (910 kg).

6. I am a scavenger that is often seen soaring in the sky in search of food.

Answers

Make Words

The **pangolin** – also known as a scaly anteater – is an African mammal covered with heavy scales. It has long claws that it uses to tear open termite mounds and a long sticky tongue for lapping up insects. It is related to the North American armadillo. Like the armadillo, it rolls itself into a ball to protect itself when threatened.

How many words can you make from the letters in its name?

_____   _____

_____   _____

_____   _____

_____   _____

_____   _____

_____   _____

_____   _____

_____   _____

Picture Scramble

Place the numbers 1 through 9 in the lettered boxes
on the right to create the image on the left.

PUFF ADDER

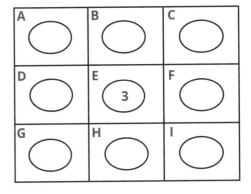

A	B	C
D	E 3	F
G	H	I

AFRICAN BLACK CRAKE

1.	2.	3.
4.	5.	6.
7. 8.	9.	

A	B	C
D	E 8	F
G	H	I

BARBARY SHEEP

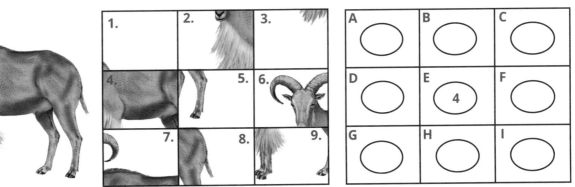

A	B	C
D	E 4	F
G	H	I

13

Be An Artist

Draw this elephant by copying it one square at a time.

African elephants
are the world's largest land mammal. These giant vegetarians can weigh as much as 24,000 lbs. (11,000 kg) and be up to 13 ft. (4 m) tall! Adult elephants have no natural predators and can live up to 82 years.

Color Me

Chameleons have the ability to change color because of special skin cells. They can use this ability to blend in to their surroundings and hide from predators, but their naturally greenish brown color usually provides the best camouflage. Scientists believe they may also change colors to reflect their moods and send "signals" to other chameleons.

Use the Color Key to help you color the picture of the chameleon.

Color Key

Word Search

Find the names of these African hoofed mammals.

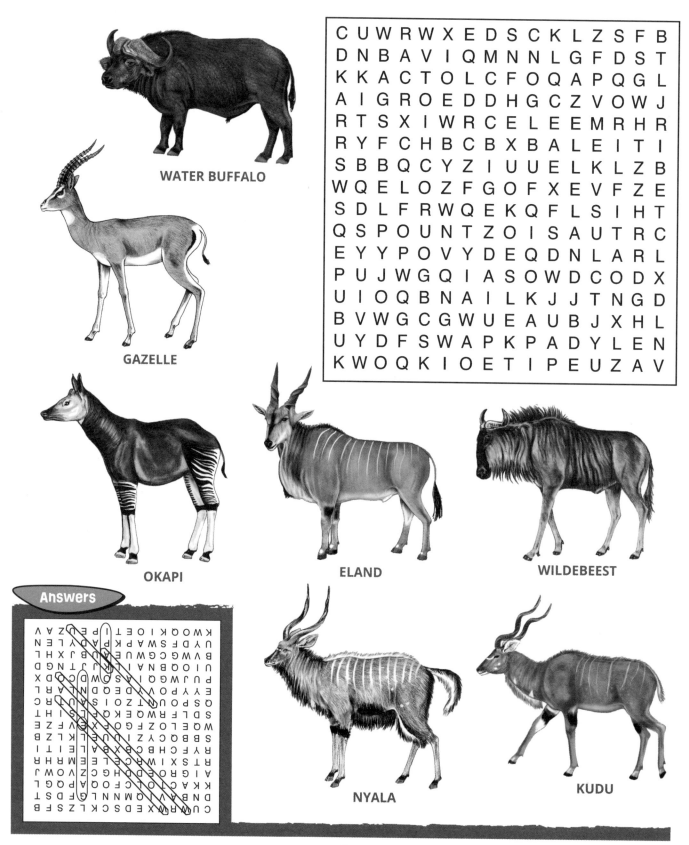

WATER BUFFALO

GAZELLE

C U W R W X E D S C K L Z S F B
D N B A V I Q M N N L G F D S T
K K A C T O L C F O Q A P Q G L
A I G R O E D D H G C Z V O W J
R T S X I W R C E L E E M R H R
R Y F C H B C B X B A L E I T I
S B B Q C Y Z I U U E L K L Z B
W Q E L O Z F G O F X E V F Z E
S D L F R W Q E K Q F L S I H T
Q S P O U N T Z O I S A U T R C
E Y Y P O V Y D E Q D N L A R L
P U J W G Q I A S O W D C O D X
U I O Q B N A I L K J J T N G D
B V W G C G W U E A U B J X H L
U Y D F S W A P K P A D Y L E N
K W O Q K I O E T I P E U Z A V

OKAPI

ELAND

WILDEBEEST

NYALA

KUDU

Name Scramble

Unscramble the letters to form the names
of these nearshore birds

1. **PNUEGIN**

2. **EPLAICN**

3. **LUGL**

4. **ERHNO**

5. **EOGOS**

6. **TSROK**

7. **NCAJAA**

8. **NOOCMRRAT**

Color Me

A **giraffe's** color can vary from light tan to nearly black. These differences between giraffes may be due to their habitat and food source. The African giraffe's spotted coat helps camouflage it among the trees and shrubs of the savanna. However, scientists believe the patches are also part of a system of blood vessels beneath the skin that help the giraffe regulate body temperature.

Use the Color Key to help you color the picture of the giraffe.

Color Key

Maze

Zebras live in large herds. One of the main benefits of living in herds is that there are many more eyes on the lookout for predators like lions and leopards.

Help the zebra find its way back to the herd.

ENTER

Animal Tracks

Match the track to the correct mammal.

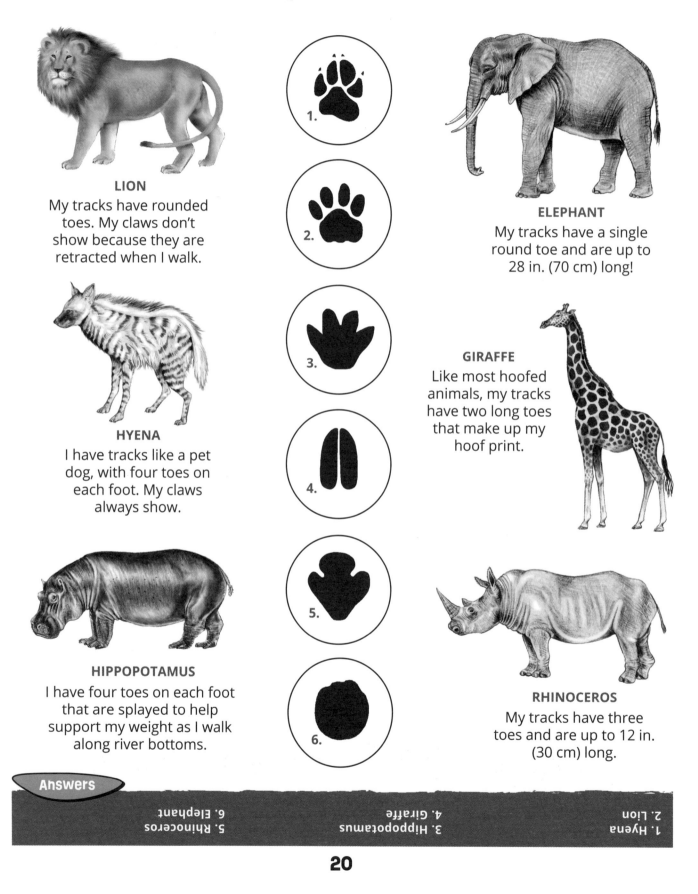

LION
My tracks have rounded toes. My claws don't show because they are retracted when I walk.

ELEPHANT
My tracks have a single round toe and are up to 28 in. (70 cm) long!

HYENA
I have tracks like a pet dog, with four toes on each foot. My claws always show.

GIRAFFE
Like most hoofed animals, my tracks have two long toes that make up my hoof print.

HIPPOPOTAMUS
I have four toes on each foot that are splayed to help support my weight as I walk along river bottoms.

RHINOCEROS
My tracks have three toes and are up to 12 in. (30 cm) long.

1. 2. 3. 4. 5. 6.

Answers

Color Me

Use the Color Key to help you color the pictures below.

The **leopard** is a large carnivore with a long body and a broad head. Its coats ranges from light yellow in warm, dry habitats to red-orange in dense forests. Its dark, irregular spots are called rosettes.

Color Key

The **lilac-breasted roller** is one of Africa's most colorful birds. It prefers open woodland and savanna.

Color Key

Name Match

Draw a line between the animal and its name.

1.

2.

3.

4.

RED-BILLED HORNBILL

PATAS MONKEY

MEERKAT

AFRICAN JACANA

BLACK MAMBA

AFRICAN WILD DOG

OSTRICH

RED-HEADED AGAMA

5.

6.

7.

8.

Word Search

Find the names of these African animals.

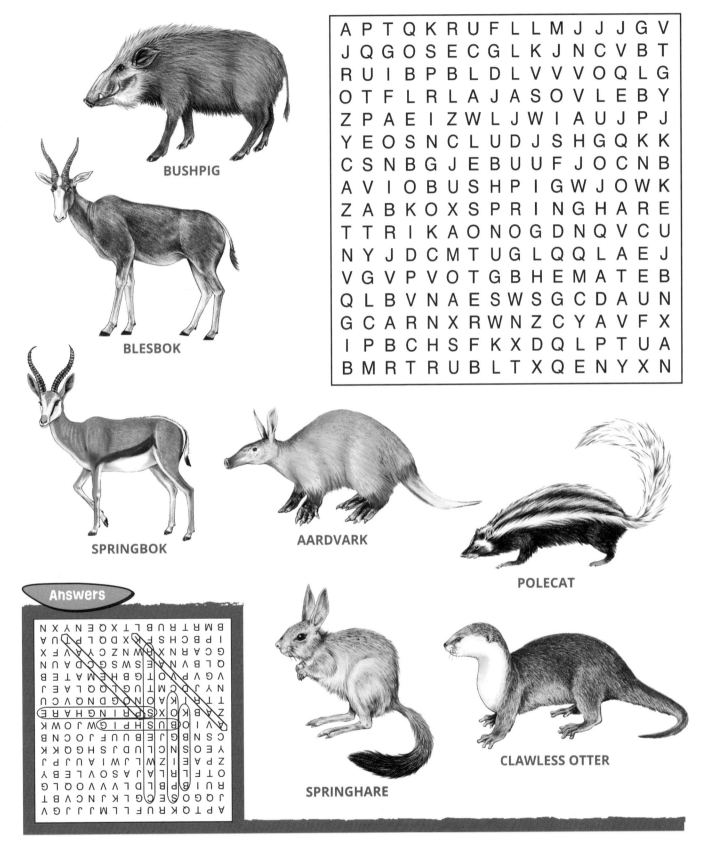

BUSHPIG

BLESBOK

```
A P T Q K R U F L L M J J J G V
J Q G O S E C G L K J N C V B T
R U I B P B L D L V V V O Q L G
O T F L R L A J A S O V L E B Y
Z P A E I Z W L J W I A U J P J
Y E O S N C L U D J S H G Q K K
C S N B G J E B U U F J O C N B
A V I O B U S H P I G W J O W K
Z A B K O X S P R I N G H A R E
T T R I K A O N O G D N Q V C U
N Y J D C M T U G L Q Q L A E J
V G V P V O T G B H E M A T E B
Q L B V N A E S W S G C D A U N
G C A R N X R W N Z C Y A V F X
I P B C H S F K X D Q L P T U A
B M R T R U B L T X Q E N Y X N
```

SPRINGBOK

AARDVARK

POLECAT

Answers

CLAWLESS OTTER

SPRINGHARE

Shadow Know-How

Can you identify these African animals?

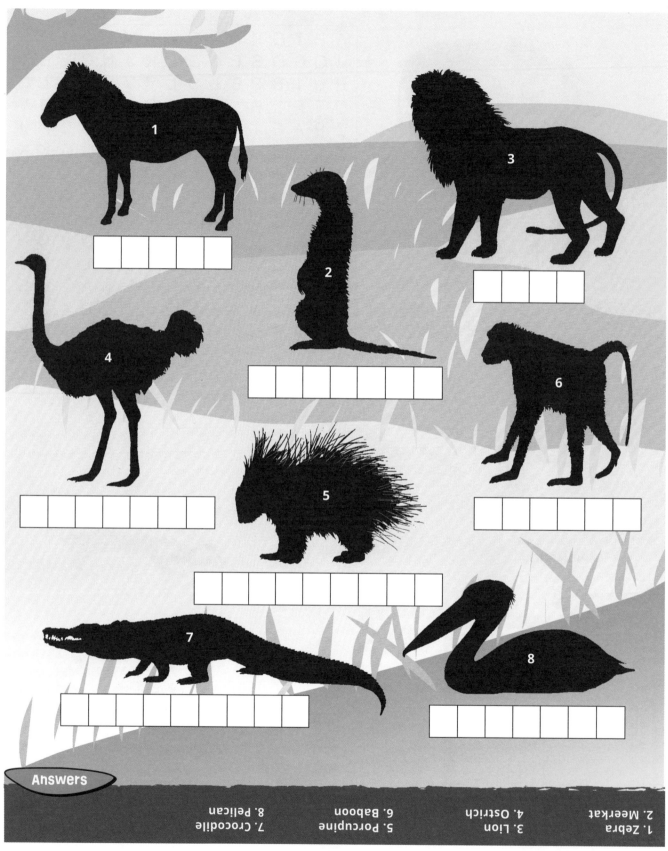

Oddball Out

In each row, circle the animal that is different from the others.

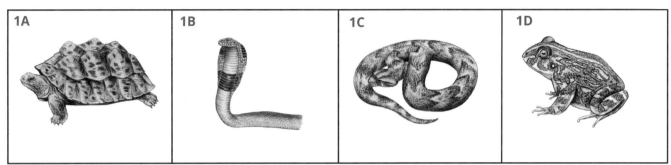

1A **1B** **1C** **1D**

Three of these are reptiles; one is not.

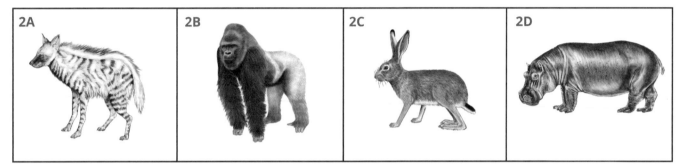

2A **2B** **2C** **2D**

Three of these are herbivores (plant-eaters); one is not.

3A **3B** **3C** **3D**

Three of these birds are owls; one is not.

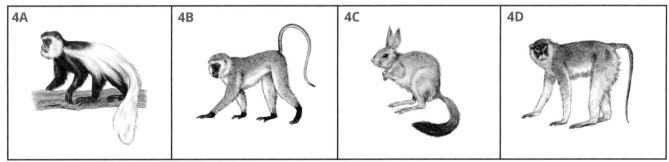

4A **4B** **4C** **4D**

Three of these mammals are monkeys; one is not.

Be An Artist

Draw this spotted hyena by copying it one square at a time.

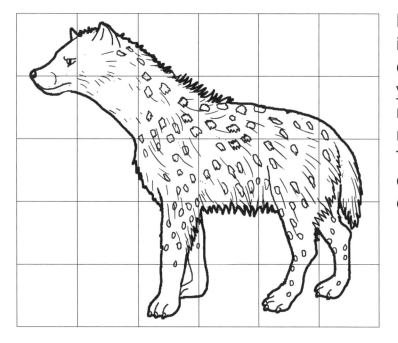

Hyenas are carnivores that hunt in packs like wolves. The pack communicates using high-pitched yapping and barking sounds that mimic laughter, giving them the nickname "laughing hyenas." They have powerful jaws and can crush and eat the bones of any animal.

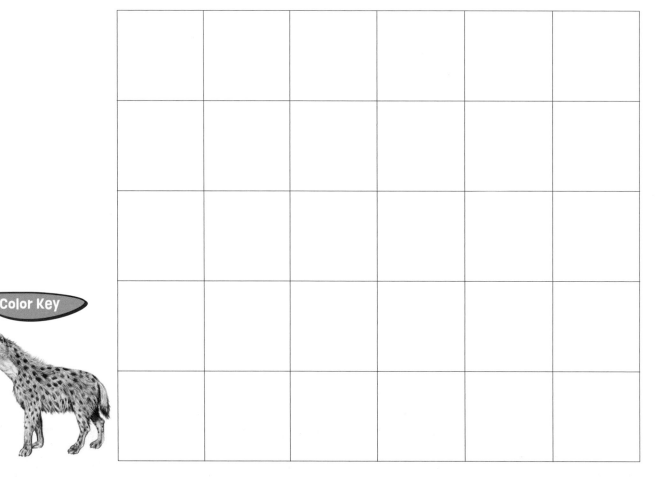

Color Key

Make Words

The **wildebeest** – also called a gnu – is one of the most common animals on the African savanna. It normally lives in small herds of 10 to 30, but once a year up to 500,000 undergo a massive migration in search of new grazing lands.

How many words can you make from the letters in its name?

_____   _____

_____   _____

_____   _____

_____   _____

_____   _____

_____   _____

_____   _____

_____   _____

Picture Scramble

Place the numbers 1 through 9 in the lettered boxes
on the right to create the image on the left.

**AFRICAN
BULLFROG**

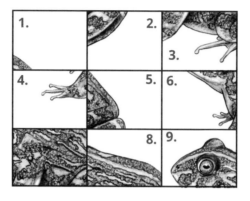

1.	2.	
		3.
4.	5.	6.
	8.	9.

A	B	C
D	E (7)	F
G	H	I

**GREAT WHITE
PELICAN**

1.	2.	3.
4.	5.	6.
7.	8.	9.

A	B	C
D	E (1)	F
G	H	I

STRIPED HYENA

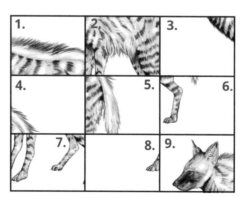

1.	2.	3.
4.	5.	6.
7.	8.	9.

A	B	C
D	E (2)	F
G	H	I

Word Search

Find the names of these African birds.

N Z W S T M W U L A Y L C C K R
E W C E B F T B U S T A R D N E
B H C R E S T E D B A R B E T D
G E J T O E L L P V E U C X O H
S Y E U Y C T D D P F G H V N E
L Y X E B R O B W Y L L L H Y A
P M Y O A E H D A X X S O A A D
I M W Q A T S G I T Z M O X S E
C Z J C C A E M O L A V P B U D
F C E N N R Q R G J E L D H N W
Q I Y G G Y N A Y P K B E A B E
E D A P Z B M Z Z H L D I U I A
J A H X S I F M G J Z K U R R V
M J L M W R I Z K H H D M W D E
X P N E K D Z M Y L Y S V H Z R
B N V N T Z O A E P W P U B X S

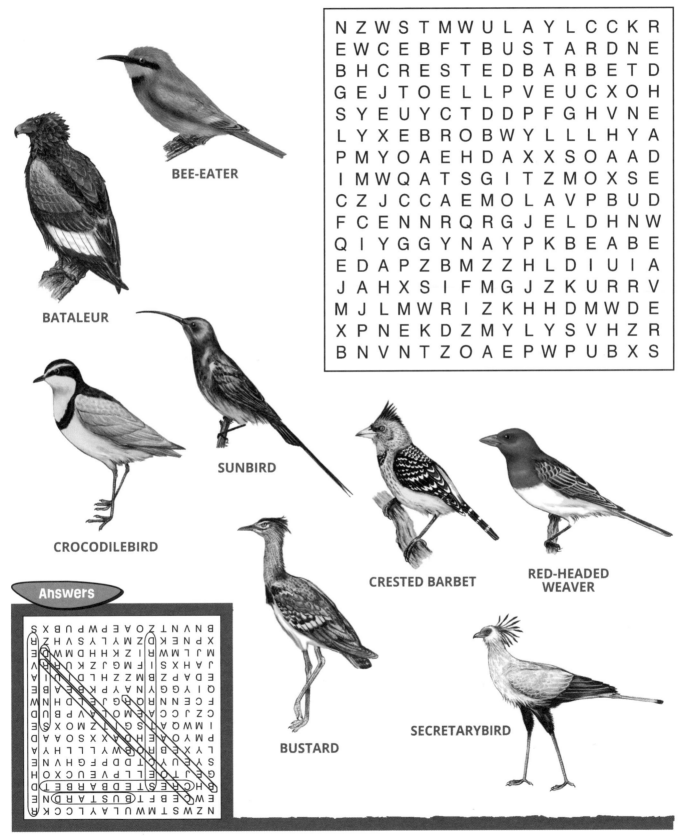

BEE-EATER

BATALEUR

SUNBIRD

CROCODILEBIRD

CRESTED BARBET

RED-HEADED WEAVER

BUSTARD

SECRETARYBIRD

Answers

29

Maze

The **black mamba** is the fastest snake on Earth. It can move at up to 12 mph (20 kph). It is also the longest venomous African snake, reaching up to 14 ft. (4.3 m) in length. It is named for the black inner lining of its mouth, which it often displays before striking.

Help this black mamba find some eggs to eat.

ENTER

Who Am I?

Name these African animals.

1. I rarely travel far from cities or towns.

_____

4. I am one of the most well known aerial scavengers, always on the lookout for a meal.

_____

2. I'm named for my massive curving beak.

_____

5. I am a vegetarian that feeds primarily on leaves and grasses in the jungles of central Africa.

_____

3. I am a very quick and agile predator and often prey on poisonous snakes like cobras.

_____

6. I like to hang around in mud wallows and am often seen running with my tail in the air.

_____

Answers

Wildlife Respect

In wild spaces, humans are the visitors. We are lucky to be able to observe animals in their natural habitats. Along with that privilege comes a responsibility to respect the animals we see, as well as their homes. The best way to learn about wildlife is by quietly watching. Though the possibility of getting a better look – or a better photo – can be tempting, getting too close can be stressful to a wild animal.

Here are some ways you can help reduce the number of disruptive human encounters that wild animals experience:

1. Know the site before you go.

2. When taking photos, do not use a flash, which can disturb animals.

3. Give animals room to move and act naturally.

4. Visit after breakfast and before dinner when wild animals are less active.

5. Do not touch or disturb the animals.

6. Do not feed the animals.

7. Store your food and take your trash with you.

8. Read and respect signs.

9. Do not make quick movements or loud noises.

10. Report any encounters with dangerous animals.